Mini Sweets

Mini Sweets

This edition published in 2012

LOVE FOOD is an imprint of Parragon Books Ltd

Parragon
Chartist House
15–17 Trim Street
Bath BA1 1HA, UK

www.parragon.com/lovefood

ISBN: 978-1-78186-379-4

Printed in China

Created and produced by Pene Parker and Becca Spry
Author and home economist: Sunil Vijayakar
Photographer: Karen Thomas

Notes for the reader

This book uses both metric and imperial measurements. Follow the same units of measurements
throughout; do not mix metric and imperial. All spoon measurements are level: teaspoons are
assumed to be 5 ml, and tablespoons are assumed to be 15 ml. Unless otherwise stated, milk is
assumed to be full fat, and eggs and individual fruits are medium.

The times given are an approximate guide only. Preparation times differ according to the
techniques used by different people and the cooking times may also vary from those given.
Optional ingredients, variations or serving suggestions have not been included in the calculations.

Recipes using raw or very lightly cooked eggs should be avoided by infants, the elderly, pregnant
women, convalescents and anyone suffering from an illness. Pregnant and breastfeeding women are
advised to avoid eating peanuts and peanut products. Sufferers from nut allergies should be aware
that some of the ready-made ingredients used in the recipes in this book may contain nuts. Always
check the packaging before use.

Contents

Introduction

Everybody loves a sweet treat, and what could be nicer than being able to make, sample and enjoy a variety of bite-sized sweets that are easy to prepare, look terrific and won't leave you feeling guilty about over-indulging in our health-conscious society?

Ingredients

Chocolate

Plain, milk and white chocolate and cocoa powder are used in the recipes in this book. There are many brands and varieties of chocolate, and it is always worth buying the best you can afford. I recommend tasting it to see which you like the best – look for appearance, aroma, flavour, texture and after-taste.

Plain chocolate contains at least 35 per cent cocoa solids, and can contain over 70 per cent. The higher the percentage of cocoa solids, the richer the flavour. Milk chocolate usually contains at least 25 per cent cocoa solids, and tends to consist of cocoa butter, milk, sugar and flavourings. White chocolate is made from cocoa butter, milk solids, sugar, flavourings such as vanilla, and emulsifiers such as lecithin.

Eggs

Eggs are basic ingredients in baking. They serve many functions in sweets, providing structure, colour, texture, flavour and moisture. Use organic or free-range eggs if possible. Always check the dates on the carton, and use eggs that are fresh. Do not use egg substitutes in place of fresh eggs and always store your eggs in a cool place, but not in the fridge.

Flour

Plain flour and self-raising flour are both used in this book. Plain flour (also known as all-purpose flour) has a medium gluten content. It can be white or wholemeal and does not contain a raising agent. Self-raising flour can be white, brown or wholemeal, and has baking powder added. It is used where a cake, biscuit or bread needs to rise; for example, for the mini chocolate-dipped doughnuts (see page 58). Don't substitute wholemeal flour in these recipes as it is heavier and dense, and will change the texture of the sweet.

Butter

All the recipes in this book use unsalted butter. This enables you to control the amount of salt in the sweet. Do not replace butter with margarine or butter substitutes, as this would affect the texture and flavour of the sweet.

Gelatine

This book uses both powdered and leaf gelatine. For powdered gelatine, scoop the powder into a measuring teaspoon so it is level with the spoon, then sprinkle it over your liquid. If specks remain on the surface of the liquid, gently stir them in using a teaspoon. For leaf gelatine, ensure the gelatine is completely submerged in the liquid. Allow the gelatine to soak for 10 minutes (it forms a sponge-like mixture).

Dried fruits and nuts

Dried fruits and nuts give sweets colour, texture and flavour. Many dried fruits and nuts are used in these recipes, including sultanas, dried cranberries, dried apricots, ground almonds, hazelnuts, cashew nuts, pistahio nuts, flaked almonds, walnuts and pecans. Most of these can be substituted for one another in these recipes if you prefer.

Sugar and spice

The spices and flavourings used in the recipes in this book include chilli powder, ground ginger, ground cardamom seeds, vanilla extract, peppermint extract and strawberry and raspberry flavourings.

Make sure your spices are fresh. They should be stored in airtight containers once the packets are opened. Sugars add colour, flavour, sweetness and moisture.

The recipes in this book use muscovado, granulated, caster, soft brown and icing sugars and syrups, such as golden syrup and glucose syrup.

Always try to have these sugars and spices in your storecupboard at home.

Equipment

Here are some essential pieces of equipment for making mini sweets:

Heavy-based saucepans
Good heavy-based saucepans in various sizes are crucial for working with sugar and chocolate, so they don't burn on the bottom of the pan.

Baking trays and tins
You'll need non-stick baking trays of various sizes, including 30 x 20 cm/12 x 8 inches, 28 x 18 cm/ 11 x 7 inches and 20 cm/8 inches square ones.

Heavy duty metal baking trays are best, as they don't buckle from the heat of the oven. Make sure you buy ones that fit in your oven.

You'll also need a square loose-bottomed cake tin measuring 20 cm/8 inches and another measuring 17 cm/7 inches, as well as a heavy 20-cm/8-inch square baking tin and a 24-cm/10-inch square baking tin for fudge.

Be sure to buy good quality baking trays and tins – it really is worth it as they last a lifetime if they are well looked after.

Non-stick baking paper
Non-stick baking paper is invaluable for lining baking trays and tins.

Sugar thermometer

A sugar thermometer is essential for cooking sugar mixtures to a particular desired temperature. It will read between 37.7°C/100°F and 204.5°C/400°F in two-degree increments.

Make sure that the thermometer takes the temperature of the mixture in the pan and not of the bottom of the pan to get an accurate reading.

Electric mixer

The electric stand mixer is one of the most important tools for making sweets. It allows you to be hands-free while adding different ingredients or attending to other tasks as your ingredients are mixing.

Electric handheld whisk

The electric handheld whisk is crucial for whisking, blending and mixing ingredients for specific tasks, such as making macaroons.

Food Processor

The food processor is one of the most useful tools in the kitchen. It's terrific for chopping and grinding nuts as well as for blending mixtures.

Digital scales and measuring cups

It is essential to have digital scales, measuring cups and a set of measuring spoons.

Microplane graters

Invest in stainless steel, razor-sharp graters in various sizes for different tasks, such as finely grating lemon rind and making chocolate curls.

Spatula

A heat-resistant spatula is invaluable for stirring mixtures as they cook.

Kitchen timer

Kitchen timers come in all shapes and sizes. Use a timer that is easy to read. Always set the timer for the least amount of time called for in the recipe – you can add more time if needed.

Cooking techniques

Here are a few techniques used in the recipes in this book:

Melting chocolate

Put roughly chopped or broken chocolate in a sturdy heatproof bowl that will fit sungly over a heavy-based saucepan, so that no heat or steam can escape. Bring the saucepan of water to a gentle simmer, then set the bowl over it and continue simmering over a low heat until the chocolate has melted. Keep the water level in the pan at no more than 2.5 cm/1 inch deep and do not allow the bottom of the bowl containing the chocolate to touch the water or you may burn the chocolate. Once the chocolate has melted, use a rubber spatula to mix it until it is smooth. If you prefer to melt chocolate in a microwave, put the broken chocolate in a microwave-proof bowl and melt it on the lowest power in 30-second bursts. Stir with a rubber spatula after each burst.

Whisking eggs and egg whites

To whisk eggs to their full volume, it is best to have them at room temperature first. Use an electric stand mixer or handheld electric whisk with a bowl that is large enough for the eggs to triple in volume. Start with a medium speed and step it up to medium–high as the eggs increase in size. When whisking egg whites, it is very important that the bowl is clean with no trace of grease or fat, or they won't whisk properly. Egg whites can be frozen for up to 3 months. To defrost, allow them to come to room temperature before using.

Whisking cream

Chilled cream whisks best, as it holds onto the air whipped into it better. Chill the bowl and beaters if you can before whisking the cream. Start whisking on a medium speed and watch carefully as it can easily be over-whisked and get too firm. If this happens, you can rectify it by adding another couple of tablespoons of cream and whisking gently until it becomes smooth.

Chopping nuts

Chop nuts on a chopping board using a chef's knife, or pulse them using a food processor.

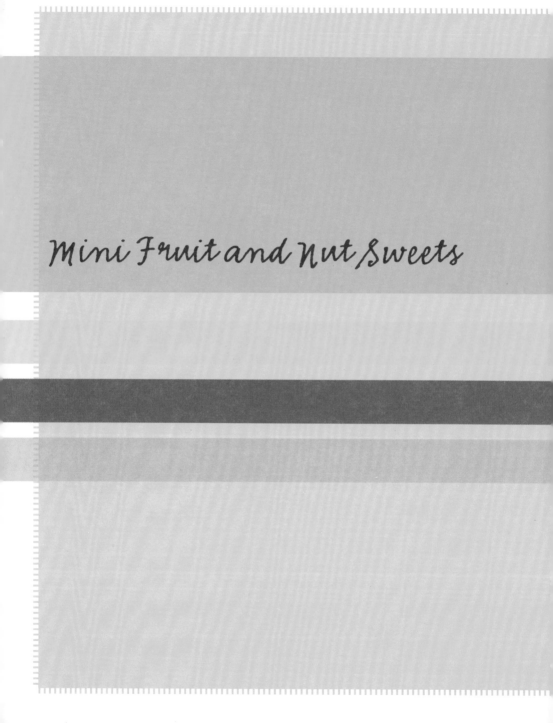

Mini Fruit and Nut Sweets

Strawberry ripple marshmallows

Makes: 32
Prep: 40 minutes
Cook: 20 minutes
Set: 1 hour

Light and fluffy, these pretty cubes of sweetness and light will put a smile on everyone's face. They are equally good made with raspberry extract instead of strawberry.

a little sunflower oil, for greasing

cornflour, for dusting

icing sugar, sifted, for dusting

11 sheets of leaf gelatine
(approximately 20 g/¾ oz)

340 ml/11½ fl oz water

1 tbsp liquid glucose

450 g/1 lb caster sugar

3 egg whites

1 tsp strawberry extract

2 tsp pink food colouring

1. Lightly brush a 30 x 20-cm/12 x 8-inch baking tray with oil, then lightly dust it with cornflour and sifted icing sugar.

2. Put the gelatine into a small bowl and add 140 ml/4½ fl oz water, making sure the gelatine is absorbed (see page 6). Set aside for 10 minutes.

3. Put the glucose, sugar and remaining 200 ml/7 fl oz water into a medium heavy-based saucepan. Bring to the boil, then reduce the heat and simmer for 15 minutes, or until the mixture reaches 127°C/260°F on a sugar thermometer. Remove from the heat, stir the gelatine mixture, then carefully spoon it into the pan; the syrup will bubble up. Pour the syrup into a measuring jug and stir.

4. Whisk the egg whites in a large, clean mixing bowl until you have stiff, moist-looking peaks, then gradually whisk in the hot syrup. The mixture will become shiny and start to thicken. Add the strawberry extract and whisk for 5–10 minutes, until the mixture is stiff enough to hold its shape on the whisk.

5. Spoon the mixture into the prepared baking tray and smooth using a wet palette knife. Sprinkle over the food colouring and use a small skewer to marble it through on the surface. Leave to set for 1 hour.

6. Loosen the marshmallow around the sides of the tray using a round-bladed knife, then turn it out onto a board. Cut it into 32 squares, then lightly dust with cornflour and sifted icing sugar. Place on a wire rack to dry. Serve immediately.

Apple and apricot fruit jellies

Makes: 30
Prep: 25 minutes
Cook: 10 minutes
Set: 3–4 hours

Called 'jujubes' in many countries, these fruity cubes are refreshing and delicious. You can change the fruit flavour simply by using a different fruit juice and jam.

450 ml/16 fl oz clear apple juice

3 tbsp powdered gelatine

400 g/14 oz caster sugar

500 g/1 lb 2 oz apricot jam

1. Put half the apple juice into a mixing bowl, then sprinkle the gelatine over the surface, making sure the powder is absorbed (see page 6). Set aside for 10 minutes.

2. Meanwhile, put the remaining apple juice and half the sugar into a heavy-based saucepan. Boil, stirring, for 5–6 minutes, or until the sugar has dissolved. Whisk in the jam, then return to the boil and cook for 3–4 minutes, until the mixture is thick and syrupy. Whisk the gelatine into the syrup until it dissolves.

3. Pour the mixture through a fine-mesh sieve into a bowl. Transfer it to a 25 x 17-cm/10 x 7-inch non-stick cake tin. Chill in the fridge for 3–4 hours, or until set.

4. Spread the remaining sugar over a large baking tray. Cut the fruit jelly into 30 squares and remove from the tin using a palette knife. Toss in the sugar to coat just before serving. Serve or store in an airtight container in a cool, dry place for up to 5 days.

Raspberry coconut ice

Makes: 20
Prep: 30 minutes
Set: 3 hours

A no-cook sweet treat that is perfect to make with the kids. This is a lovely gift when wrapped in cellophane bags or little gift boxes.

a little sunflower oil, for greasing

325 g/11½ oz icing sugar, sifted, plus extra if needed

325 g/11½ oz sweetened desiccated coconut

400 g/14 oz canned sweetened full-fat condensed milk

1 tsp vanilla extract

55 g/2 oz raspberries

½ tsp pink food colouring

1 tsp raspberry extract

1. Lightly brush a 20-cm/8-inch square baking tin with oil. Line the base with non-stick baking paper.

2. Put half the sifted icing sugar and half the coconut into one mixing bowl and put the other half into a second bowl. Stir the contents of each bowl, then make a well in the centre.

3. Add half the condensed milk and half the vanilla to each of the coconut mixtures and stir. Press one of the mixtures into the prepared tin and level using a spatula.

4. Put the raspberries into a blender and whizz to a purée. Push this through a sieve into a bowl to remove the seeds. Add the purée, food colouring and raspberry extract to the remaining coconut mixture. Add more sifted icing sugar if the mixture is too wet.

5. Spread the pink coconut ice over the white coconut layer, cover, then chill in the fridge for 3 hours, or until set.

6. Lift the coconut ice out of the tin, peel off the paper and cut into 20 squares. Store in an airtight container in a cool, dry place for up to 5 days.

Mini toffee apples

Makes: 12
Prep: 25 minutes
Cook: 20-25 minutes

Nothing beats the crunch of a homemade toffee apple on an autumnal evening. Pack these mini treats for an extra surprise at a Bonfire Night get-together.

3 large red apples

juice of 1 lemon

100 g/3½ oz caster sugar

175 ml/6 fl oz water

15 g/½ oz unsalted butter

a few drops of red food colouring

1. Put a bowl of iced water in the fridge. Using a melon scoop, scoop out 12 balls from the apples, making sure each ball has some red skin on it. Push a small skewer into each ball through the red skin. Squeeze over the lemon juice to prevent the apple from discolouring and set aside.

2. Put the sugar, water and butter into a medium heavy-based saucepan. Heat gently until the sugar has dissolved, tilting the pan to mix the ingredients together. Increase the heat and boil rapidly for 12–15 minutes, or until the mixture reaches 160°C/320°F on a sugar thermometer and is deep golden. Turn off the heat, stir in the food colouring and allow the bubbles to subside.

3. Remove the bowl of iced water from the fridge. Working as quickly as possible, dip the apples into the toffee one at a time, rotating them a few times to get an even coating, then drop them into the iced water for 30 seconds. Serve immediately.

Pistachio and apricot nougat

Makes: 16
Prep: 30 minutes
Cook: 15 minutes
Set: 8-10 hours

A confection made from boiled honey and sugar syrup mixed with beaten egg white, nuts and dried fruit. It is associated with the French town of Montélimar, where it has been made since the 18th century. Enjoy it as an after dinner sweet with coffee, crumble it over ice cream or use it in desserts and puddings.

edible rice paper

250 g/9 oz caster sugar

125 ml/4 fl oz liquid glucose

85 g/3 oz runny honey

2 tbsp water

a pinch of salt

1 egg white

½ tsp vanilla extract

60 g/2¼ oz unsalted butter, softened and diced

50 g/1¾ oz pistachio nuts, roughly chopped

50 g/1¾ oz ready-to-eat dried apricots, finely chopped

1. Line a 17-cm/7-inch square loose-bottomed cake tin with cling film, leaving an overhang. Line the base with edible rice paper.

2. Put the sugar, glucose, honey, water and salt into a heavy-based saucepan. Heat gently until the sugar has dissolved, tilting the pan to mix the ingredients together. Increase the heat and boil for 8 minutes, or until the mixture reaches 121°C/250°F on a sugar thermometer.

3. Put the egg white into an electric mixer or use a handheld whisk, and beat until firm. Gradually pour in a quarter of the hot syrup in a thin stream while still beating the egg. Continue beating for 5 minutes, until the mixture is stiff enough to hold its shape on the whisk.

4. Put the pan containing the remaining syrup over a gentle heat for 2 minutes, or until the mixture reaches 143°C/290°F on a sugar thermometer. Gradually pour the syrup over the egg mixture while beating.

5. Add the vanilla and butter and beat for a further 5 minutes. Add the pistachios and apricots and stir.

6. Pour the mixture into the tin and level using a palette knife. Cover with edible rice paper and chill in the fridge for 8-10 hours, or until fairly firm.

7. Lift the nougat out of the tin and cut into 16 squares. Serve or store in an airtight container in the fridge for up to 5 days.

Peanut butter and chocolate candy balls

Makes: 36
Prep: 25 minutes
Cook: 5 minutes
Set: 4–6 hours

This recipe uses plain chocolate to coat the peanut candy balls, but if you prefer you can use milk or white chocolate, or a mixture of the three.

250 g/9 oz smooth peanut butter

55 g/2 oz unsalted butter

20 g/¼ oz rice pops

200 g/7 oz icing sugar

200 g/7 oz plain chocolate, roughly chopped

1. Line 2 baking trays with non-stick baking paper. Melt the peanut butter and butter together in a heavy-based saucepan.

2. Put the rice pops and icing sugar into a large mixing bowl. Pour in the melted butter mixture, then stir. When cool enough to handle, using the palms of your hands, roll the mixture into 2.5-cm/1-inch balls, then put them on the prepared baking trays and chill in the fridge for 3–4 hours, or until firm.

3. Put the chocolate in a heatproof bowl, set the bowl over a saucepan of gently simmering water and heat until melted.

4. Using a teaspoon, dip the balls into the chocolate one by one, making sure they are covered completely, then lift them out and return them to the baking trays. Chill in the fridge for 1–2 hours, or until set. Serve or store in an airtight container in the fridge for up to 5 days.

Sea-salted pecan candies

Makes: 12
Prep: 15 minutes
Cook: 10–15 minutes
Set: 10 minutes

You can replace the pecan nuts with walnuts, whole peeled almonds or cashew nuts if you prefer.

55 g/2 oz pecan nuts

300 g/10½ oz caster sugar

175 ml/6 fl oz water

2 tsp sea salt

1. Preheat the grill to medium.

2. Put the pecans in a baking tray and toast them under the grill for 3–4 minutes, or until golden, shaking them halfway through. Divide the nuts between the sections of a 12-section silicone mini muffin tray.

3. Put the sugar and water into a heavy-based saucepan. Heat gently until the sugar has dissolved, tilting the pan to mix the ingredients together, until the mixture reaches an even light brown colour. Continue cooking until it is a slightly deeper brown, watching it carefully so it doesn't burn. Scatter in the sea salt.

4. Transfer the mixture into a jug and quickly pour it into the sections of the mini muffin tray. Leave to cool for 10 minutes, until the sweets set and harden. Turn the candies out of the tray. Store in an airtight container in a cool, dry place for up to 5 days.

Mini Toffee and Fudge Sweets

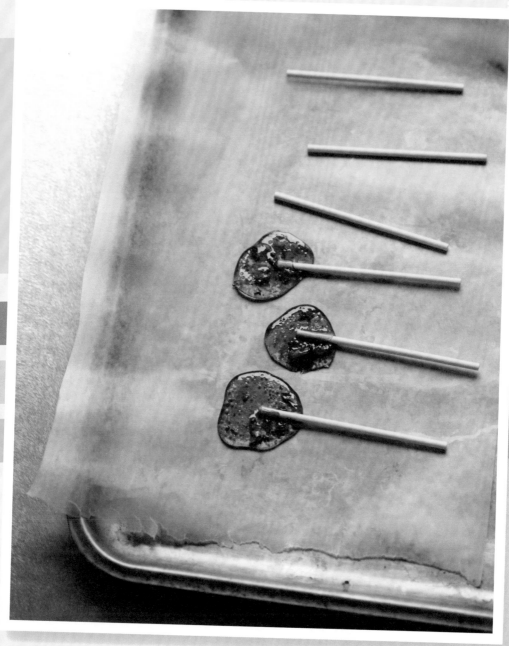

Toffee popcorn

Makes: 200 g/7 oz
Prep: 15 minutes
Cook: 5–10 minutes

This popcorn is fun to make as a treat for children's birthday parties. For adults, sprinkle on a little cayenne pepper to get a sweet and spicy kick.

25 g/1 oz unsalted butter

55 g/2 oz popping corn

TOFFEE COATING

40 g/1½ oz unsalted butter

55 g/2 oz soft dark brown sugar

2 tbsp golden syrup

1. Melt the butter in a large heavy-based saucepan. Sprinkle in the popping corn and swirl the pan to coat the corn evenly.

2. Cover the pan with a tight-fitting lid, reduce the heat to low and let the corn start popping. Shake the pan a couple of times to move the unpopped pieces to the bottom. As soon as the popping stops, take the pan off the heat and leave it to stand, covered.

3. For the toffee coating, melt the butter in a medium heavy-based saucepan. Add the sugar and syrup and cook over a high heat, stirring, for 1–2 minutes, or until the sugar has dissolved.

4. Pour the toffee coating over the popped corn, replace the lid on the pan and shake well. Allow to cool slightly, then serve immediately.

Honeycomb brittle

Makes: approx 20
Prep: 15 minutes
Cook: 10–15 minutes
Set: 5 minutes

Known as hokey-pokey in Australia, this light and crunchy brittle is perfect broken into bite-size pieces or crushed over ice cream.

a little sunflower oil, for greasing

175 g/6 oz caster sugar

100 g/3½ oz golden syrup

100 g/3½ oz unsalted butter, diced

2 tsp bicarbonate of soda

1. Lightly brush a 20-cm/8-inch square baking tin with oil.

2. Put the sugar, syrup and butter into a large heavy-based saucepan. Heat gently until the sugar has dissolved, tilting the pan to mix the ingredients together. Increase the heat and boil rapidly for 4–5 minutes, or until the mixture goes a light golden colour.

3. Add the bicarbonate of soda and stir for a few seconds; be careful as the mixture will expand and bubble.

4. Pour the mixture into the prepared tin. Leave to cool for 5 minutes, or until set. Break the brittle into shards. Store in an airtight container in a cool, dry place for up to 2 weeks.

Sesame, marshmallow and cranberry squares

Makes: 20
Prep: 15 minutes
Cook: 20 minutes

These are best baked in advance. They make a great teatime treat or lunchbox filler.

150 g/5½ oz medium oatmeal

55 g/2 oz sesame seeds

40 g/1½ oz light brown sugar

35 g/1¼ oz mini marshmallows

70 g/2½ oz dried cranberries

8 tbsp runny honey

5 tbsp sunflower oil, plus extra for greasing

a few drops of vanilla extract

1. Preheat the oven to 160°C /325°F/Gas Mark 3. Lightly brush a 28 x 18-cm/11 x 7-inch baking tin with oil. Line the base with non-stick baking paper.

2. Put the oatmeal, sesame seeds, sugar, marshmallows and cranberries into a mixing bowl and stir. Make a well in the centre, add the honey, oil and vanilla extract then stir again.

3. Press the mixture into the prepared tin and level using a metal spoon. Bake in the preheated oven for 20 minutes, or until golden and bubbling.

4. Leave to cool in the tin for 10 minutes, then cut into small squares. Leave to cool completely before turning out of the tin. Store in an airtight container in a cool, dry place for up to 2 days.

Cashew nut brittle

Makes: approx 20
Prep: 15 minutes
Cook: 25–30 minutes

This is a wonderful, buttery brittle that is easy to make and wows everyone! You could use roasted peanuts instead of cashews, if you prefer.

150 g/5½ oz roasted, salted cashew nuts

350 g/12 oz caster sugar

¼ tsp cream of tartar

175 ml/6 fl oz water

15 g/½ oz unsalted butter

1. Line a 20-cm/8-inch square baking tin with non-stick baking paper.

2. Spread the cashew nuts over the baking tin in a thin, even layer.

3. Put the sugar, cream of tartar and water into a heavy-based saucepan. Bring to a gentle boil over a medium heat, stirring all the time.

4. Reduce the heat to low and simmer for 20–25 minutes without stirring, until the mixture reaches 143°C/290°F on a sugar thermometer. Stir in the butter, then carefully drizzle the caramel over the nuts. Leave to cool completely.

5. Break the brittle into shards. Serve or store in an airtight container in a cool, dry place for up to 2 days.

Chikki brittle pops

Makes: 12
Prep: 25 minutes
Cook: 25–30 minutes
Set: 5 minutes

These individual candy and nut 'lollipops' have an exotic flavour and texture that will impress kids and adults alike.

250 g/9 oz caster sugar

¼ tsp cream of tartar

150 ml/5 fl oz water

2 tbsp pistachio nuts, finely chopped

1 tbsp ready-to-eat dried apricots, finely chopped

1 tbsp dried rose petals (optional)

a large pinch of ground cardamom seeds

1. Line a large baking tray with baking paper. Put 12 lollipop sticks on the prepared tray, spaced well apart.

2. Put the sugar, cream of tartar and water into a heavy-based saucepan. Bring to a gentle boil over a medium heat, stirring all the time.

3. Reduce the heat to low and simmer for 20–25 minutes without stirring, until the mixture reaches 143°C/290°F on a sugar thermometer.

4. Remove the pan from the heat and stir in the pistachios, apricots, rose petals and ground cardamom.

5. Working quickly, spoon a large teaspoonful of the syrup onto one end of each lollipop stick. Leave to set for 5 minutes, until hard. Store in an airtight container in a cool, dry place for up to 2 weeks.

Vanilla fudge

Makes: 16
Prep: 15 minutes
Cook: 10–15 minutes
Set: 1 hour

Just five simple ingredients and you can make the creamiest vanilla fudge ever. A guaranteed hit! Be careful when you stir the fudge, as the mixture is very hot.

a little sunflower oil, for greasing

450 g/1 lb caster sugar

85 g/3 oz unsalted butter

150 ml/5 fl oz full-fat milk

150 ml/5 fl oz evaporated milk

2 tsp vanilla extract

1. Lightly brush a 20-cm/8-inch square baking tin with oil. Line it with non-stick baking paper, snipping diagonally into the corners, then pressing the paper into the tin so that the base and sides are lined

2. Put the sugar, butter, milk and evaporated milk into a heavy-based saucepan. Heat gently, stirring, until the sugar has dissolved.

3. Increase the heat and boil for 12–15 minutes, or until the mixture reaches 116°C/240°F on a sugar thermometer (if you don't have a sugar thermometer, spoon a little of the syrup into some iced water; it will form a soft ball when it is ready). As the temperature rises, stir the fudge occasionally so the sugar doesn't stick and burn.

4. Remove the pan from the heat, add the vanilla and beat using a wooden spoon until thickened.

5. Pour the mixture into the prepared tin and smooth the surface using a spatula. Leave to cool for 1 hour, or until set.

6. Lift the fudge out of the tin, peel off the paper and cut into small squares. Store in an airtight container in a cool, dry place for up to 2 weeks.

Indulgent whisky fudge

Makes: 16
Prep: 15 minutes
Cook: 10–15 minutes
Set 2–3 hours

If you are a chocolate and whisky lover, this is the perfect edible treat for you. You can use a good brandy instead of whisky, if you prefer.

a little sunflower oil, for greasing

250 g/9 oz soft brown sugar

100 g/3½ oz unsalted butter, diced

400 g/14 oz canned sweetened full-fat condensed milk

2 tbsp glucose syrup

25 g/1 oz walnut pieces

150 g/5½ oz plain chocolate, roughly chopped

60 ml/2¼ fl oz Scotch whisky

1. Lightly brush a 20-cm/8-inch square baking tin with oil. Line it with non-stick baking paper, snipping diagonally into the corners, then pressing the paper into the tin so that the base and sides are lined

2. Put the sugar, butter, condensed milk and glucose into a heavy-based saucepan. Heat gently, stirring, until the sugar has dissolved.

3. Increase the heat and boil for 12–15 minutes, or until the mixture reaches 116°C/240°F on a sugar thermometer (if you don't have a sugar thermometer, spoon a little of the syrup into some iced water; it will form a soft ball when it is ready). As the temperature rises, stir the fudge occasionally so the sugar doesn't stick and burn. Remove the fudge from the heat. Add the chocolate and whisky and stir together until the chocolate has melted and the mixture is smooth.

4. Preheat the grill to medium-hot. Put the walnuts in a baking tray and toast them under the grill for 2–3 minutes, or until browned. Roughly chop them.

5. Pour the mixture into the prepared baking tin, smooth the surface using a spatula and sprinkle over the walnuts. Leave to cool for 1 hour. Cover with cling film, then chill in the fridge for 1–2 hours, or until firm. Lift the fudge out of the tin, peel off the paper and cut into small squares. Store in an airtight container in a cool, dry place for up to 2 weeks.

Chocolate Pretzel fudge squares

Makes: 16
Prep: 15 minutes
Cook: 8–10 minutes
Set: 2–3 hours

These are so easy to make. The salty pretzels counteract the rich sweetness of the chocolate and condensed milk.

175 g/6 oz mini pretzels

a little sunflower oil, for greasing

2 tbsp unsalted butter, diced

300 g/10½ oz milk chocolate chips

400 g/14 oz canned sweetened full-fat condensed milk

1 tsp vanilla extract

1. Roughly chop 55 g/2 oz of the pretzels.

2. Lightly brush a 24-cm/10-inch square baking tin with oil. Line it with non-stick baking paper, snipping diagonally into the corners, then pressing the paper into the tin so that the base and sides are lined and there is a 5-cm/2-inch overhang on all sides.

3. Put the butter, chocolate chips, condensed milk and vanilla in a heatproof bowl, set the bowl over a saucepan of gently simmering water and heat, stirring occasionally, for 8–10 minutes, or until the chocolate has just melted and the mixture is smooth and warm but not hot. Remove from the heat and stir in the chopped pretzels.

4. Pour the mixture into the prepared tin, smooth the surface using a spatula and push in the whole pretzels. Leave to cool for 1 hour. Cover with cling film, then chill in the fridge for 1–2 hours, or until firm.

5. Lift the fudge out of the tin, peel off the paper and cut it into small squares. Store in an airtight container in a cool, dry place for up to 2 weeks.

Mini Chocolate Sweets

Chocolate-coated candied orange rind

Makes: 36
Prep: 55 minutes
Cook: 1 hour
Set: 2-4 hours

Strips of candied orange rind dipped in plain chocolate make an elegant gift. Alternatively, serve them with coffee after dinner.

3 large navel oranges

200 g/7 oz granulated sugar

200 ml/7 fl oz water

200 g/7 oz plain chocolate, roughly chopped

1. Using a sharp knife, cut the rind off the oranges, then remove the white pith from the rind. Slice the rind into 36 x 6 x 1-cm/2½ x ½-inch strips, discarding any you don't need.

2. Bring a small saucepan of water to the boil, then add the orange rind and simmer for 10 minutes. Drain, then rinse under cold running water. Pour more water into the pan and bring it to the boil again, then return the rind to the pan and simmer for a further 10 minutes. Repeat this process one more time.

3. Put the sugar and water into a heavy-based saucepan. Bring it to the boil and simmer gently, stirring, for 5 minutes, or until the sugar has dissolved and the mixture has reduced a little in volume. Add the orange rind and continue simmering for 15 minutes. Transfer the candied peel to a wire rack and leave to cool for 1-2 hours, or overnight. Line a baking tray with non-stick baking paper.

4. Put the chocolate in heatproof bowl, set the bowl over a saucepan of gently simmering water and heat until melted.

5. Dip a third of the length of each candied orange strip in the chocolate and place it on the prepared baking tray. Leave to cool for 1-2 hours, or until set. Store in an airtight container in a cool, dry place for up to 5 days.

Salted caramel and chocolate bites

Makes: 20
Prep: 30 minutes
Cook: 35–40 minutes

Sea salt and caramel is a classic combination, and here it is enhanced by the addition of walnuts.

a little sunflower oil, for greasing

200 g/7 oz plain chocolate, roughly chopped

150 g/5½ oz unsalted butter

2 eggs

175 g/6 oz soft light brown sugar

55 g/2 oz plain flour

1 tsp baking powder

55 g/2 oz walnut pieces, roughly chopped

6 tbsp caramel (dulce de leche)

1 tbsp sea salt

1. Preheat the oven to 170°C/325°F/Gas Mark 3. Lightly brush a 20-cm/8-inch square baking tin with oil. Line it with non-stick baking paper, snipping diagonally into the corners, then pressing the paper into the tin so that the base and sides are lined.

2. Put 70 g/2½ oz chocolate and all the butter in a heatproof bowl, set the bowl over a saucepan of gently simmering water and heat until melted, stirring from time to time.

3. Put the eggs and sugar into a mixing bowl, then sift in the flour and baking powder. Stir in the melted chocolate mixture and beat together until blended. Add the walnuts and remaining chocolate and stir together. Pour the mixture into the prepared tin and smooth the surface using a spatula.

4. Put the caramel into a small mixing bowl and beat, then swirl it through the chocolate mixture using a fork. Scatter over the sea salt and bake in the preheated oven for 30–35 minutes, or until the cake begins to shrink slightly from the sides of the tin. Leave to cool for 1 hour.

5. Lift the cake out of the tin, peel off the paper and cut it into small squares. Store in an airtight container in a cool, dry place for up to 2 days.

White and dark chocolate-dipped strawberries

Makes: 24
Prep: 10 minutes
Cook: 3-4 minutes
Set: 1 hour

Chocolate always makes a sweet special, and in this fun, party treat it is paired with luscious strawberries. Prepare it several hours before you plan to serve it if you wish.

100 g/3½ oz plain chocolate, roughly chopped

100 g/3½ oz white chocolate, roughly chopped

24 large strawberries

1. Line a baking tray with non-stick baking paper. Put the plain chocolate and white chocolate into 2 separate heatproof bowls, set the bowls over 2 saucepans of gently simmering water and heat until melted.

2. Dip the pointed end of each strawberry into one of the melted chocolates and transfer it to the prepared baking tray. Leave to cool for 1 hour, or until set.

3. Put each strawberry in a liqueur glass or on a plate and serve immediately.

Mini cranberry and ginger florentines

Makes: 48
Prep: 30 minutes
Cook: 15–20 minutes
Set: 2 hours

These crispy and chewy bites are an Italian classic and make a marvellous present.

70 g/2½ oz muscovado sugar

55 g/2 oz runny honey

100 g/3½ oz unsalted butter, plus extra for greasing

50 g /1¾ oz desiccated coconut

70 g/2½ oz flaked almonds

1 tbsp finely chopped candied peel

1 tbsp finely chopped crystallized stem ginger

100 g/3½ oz dried cranberries

50 g/1¾ oz plain flour, plus extra for dusting

250 g/9 oz plain chocolate, roughly chopped

1. Preheat the oven to 180°C/350°F/Gas Mark 4. Lightly grease with butter 4 x 12-section mini muffin tins (the base of each cup should be 2 cm/¾ inch in diameter), then lightly dust them with flour.

2. Put the sugar, honey and butter into a heavy-based saucepan. Heat gently, stirring, until the sugar has dissolved, tilting the pan to mix the ingredients together. Stir in the coconut, almonds, candied peel, crystallized ginger, cranberries and flour.

3. Put small teaspoonfuls of the mixture into the prepared muffin tins. Bake in the preheated oven for 10–12 minutes, or until golden brown. Leave to cool in the tins for 1 hour. Using a palette knife, transfer to a wire rack to firm up.

4. Meanwhile, put the chocolate in a heatproof bowl, set the bowl over a saucepan of gently simmering water and heat until melted.

5. Dip each florentine into the melted chocolate so the base is covered. Place on a wire rack, chocolate side up, and leave to set for 1 hour. Store in an airtight container in a cool, dry place for up to 2 days.

Chocolate meringue kisses

Makes: 40
Prep: 40 minutes
Cook: 50 minutes
Set: 2 hours

Elegant little 'kisses' of melt-in-the-mouth meringue dipped in chocolate, these make a very good canapé or gift.

3 egg whites

1 tsp raspberry vinegar

150 g/5½ oz caster sugar

1 tsp cornflour

2 tbsp cocoa powder, sieved

200 g/7 oz plain chocolate, roughly chopped

1. Preheat the oven to 160°C/325°F/Gas Mark 3. Line 3 baking trays with non-stick baking paper.

2. Whisk the egg whites in a large, clean mixing bowl until you have stiff, moist-looking peaks. Gradually whisk in the vinegar and sugar, a tablespoonful at a time, until thick and glossy. Using a large metal spoon, gently fold in the cornflour and cocoa.

3. Spoon the mixture into a piping bag fitted with a large star nozzle and pipe 40 x 2.5-cm/1-inch 'kisses' onto the prepared baking trays.

4. Put the trays in the preheated oven, then immediately turn the heat down to 120°C/250°F/Gas Mark ½. Bake for 45 minutes, or until crisp on the outside. Transfer the meringues to a wire rack, still on the paper, and leave to cool for 1 hour, then peel off the paper.

5. Meanwhile, put the chocolate in heatproof bowl, set the bowl over a saucepan of gently simmering water and heat until melted.

6. Line the baking trays with more baking paper. Dip the bases of the meringue kisses in the melted chocolate and place them, chocolate side up, on the prepared baking trays. Leave to set for 1 hour. Store in an airtight container in a cool, dry place for up to 2 weeks.

Nutty peppermint bark

Makes: approx 25
Prep: 20 minutes
Cook: 3–4 minutes
Set: 30 minutes

Kids and adults alike will love this treat. If you can't get hold of peppermint candy canes, substitute them with any mint candy.

200 g/7 oz red and white striped peppermint candy canes, broken into pieces

500 g/1 lb 2 oz white chocolate, roughly chopped

100 g/3½ oz chopped mixed nuts

1. Line a 30 x 20-cm/12 x 8-inch baking tin with non-stick baking paper.

2. Put the broken candy into a large plastic food bag and seal tightly. Using a rolling pin, bash the bag until the candy is crushed into small pieces.

3. Put the chocolate in a heatproof bowl, set the bowl over a saucepan of gently simmering water and heat until melted. Remove from the heat and stir in three-quarters of the candy.

4. Pour the mixture into the prepared baking tin, smooth the surface using a spatula and sprinkle over the chopped nuts and remaining candy. Press down very slightly to ensure they stick. Cover with cling film and chill in the fridge for 30 minutes, or until firm.

5. Break the peppermint bark into small, uneven pieces. Store in an airtight container in a cool, dry place for up to 2 weeks.

Mini chocolate-dipped doughnuts

Makes: 50
Prep: 30 minutes
Cook: 1½–2 hours

These mini doughnuts can be served dusted with fine caster sugar instead of being dipped in chocolate, if you prefer.

500 g/1 lb 2 oz self-raising flour, plus extra for dusting

1 tsp baking powder

90 g/3 oz caster sugar

2 eggs

2 tbsp sunflower oil, plus extra for deep frying

200 ml/7 fl oz milk

100 g/3½ oz plain chocolate, roughly chopped

1. Lightly dust a work surface with flour. Sieve the flour and baking powder into a large mixing bowl. Add the sugar and stir.

2. Put the eggs, 2 tablespoons of oil and the milk into a separate mixing bowl and whisk together lightly, then pour this into the flour mixture. Using a wooden spoon, work the ingredients together into a smooth ball, then turn this out on to the floured work surface.

3. Using a floured rolling pin, roll the dough out to a thickness of just over 1 cm/½ inch. Flour a 4-cm/1½-inch and a 1-cm/½-inch round fondant cutter. Use the larger cutter to cut out rounds of dough, then use the smaller one to cut out the centres. Re-roll the trimmings to make more doughnuts.

4. Heat the oil for deep frying in a deep saucepan until it reaches 180°C/350°F, or until a small piece of bread dropped in sizzles immediately.

5. Line a plate with kitchen paper. Carefully lower 2–3 doughnut rings into the hot oil and fry for 3–4 minutes, until golden and cooked through. Transfer to the kitchen paper-lined plate to drain and cool. Continue cooking in batches of this size until all the doughnuts are ready.

6. Put the chocolate in a heatproof bowl, set the bowl over a saucepan of gently simmering water and heat until melted. Dip the top of the doughnuts in the melted chocolate and transfer to a wire rack for 1 hour. Serve immediately.

Chocolate moustaches

Makes: 6
Prep: 10 minutes
Cook: 3-4 minutes
Set: 1 hour

For the genteel gentleman or big kid, here's a dark and delicious moustache lollipop. These are great fun to serve at parties, and make a jolly good photo opportunity too!

250 g/9 oz plain chocolate, roughly chopped

1. Put the chocolate in a heatproof bowl, set the bowl over a saucepan of gently simmering water and heat until melted. Leave to cool for a few minutes.

2. Pour the melted chocolate into 6 x 100-ml/3 ½-fl oz moustache moulds.

3. Push a lollipop stick firmly into each moustache. Chill in the fridge for 1 hour, or until set. Gently turn out. Store in an airtight container in a cool, dry place for up to 2 weeks.

Mini After Dinner Sweets

Peppermint creams

Makes: 25
Prep: 30 minutes
Set: 25 hours

The pretty and tasty peppermint cream is an old-fashioned favourite. It's a refreshing choice for an after dinner sweet.

1 large egg white

325 g/11½ oz icing sugar, sifted, plus extra for dipping if needed

a few drops of peppermint extract

a few drops of green food colouring

100 g/3½ oz plain chocolate, roughly chopped

1. Line a baking tray with non-stick baking paper.

2. Lightly whisk the egg white in a large, clean mixing bowl until it is frothy but still translucent.

3. Add the sifted icing sugar to the egg white and stir using a wooden spoon until the mixture is stiff. Knead in the peppermint extract and food colouring.

4. Using the palms of your hands, roll the mixture into walnut-sized balls and place them on the prepared baking tray. Use a fork to flatten them; if it sticks to them, dip it in icing sugar before pressing. Put the creams in the fridge to set for 24 hours.

5. Put the chocolate in a heatproof bowl, set the bowl over a saucepan of gently simmering water and heat until melted. Dip the creams halfway in the chocolate and return to the baking tray for 1 hour, or until set. Store in an airtight container in the fridge for up to 5 days.

Plain chocolate and amaretto truffles

Makes: 12
Prep: 30 minutes
Soak: 6–8 hours
Cook: 5–10 minutes
Set: 1–2 hours

These delectable morsels are so easy to make and look really glamorous! Use any liqueur instead of the amaretto if you wish.

50 ml/2 fl oz amaretto liqueur

55 g/2 oz sultanas

100 g/3½ oz plain chocolate, roughly chopped

2 tbsp double cream

70 g/2½ oz ready-made chocolate cake or brownie, crumbled

100 g/3½ oz hazelnuts

55 g/2 oz chocolate sprinkles, to decorate

1. Put the amaretto and sultanas into a small mixing bowl, cover and leave to soak for 6–8 hours. Line a baking tray with non-stick baking paper.

2. Transfer the amaretto mixture to a food processor and whizz until puréed.

3. Put the chocolate and cream in a heatproof bowl, set the bowl over a saucepan of gently simmering water and heat until melted. Remove from the heat, add the amaretto purée and chocolate cake and stir well.

4. When cool enough to handle, using the palms of your hands, roll the mixture into truffle-sized balls and place on the prepared baking tray.

5. Preheat the grill to medium. Put the hazelnuts on a second baking tray and toast them under the grill for 2–3 minutes, or until browned, shaking them halfway through. Finely chop them.

6. Spread the chocolate sprinkles onto one plate and the hazelnuts onto another. Roll half the truffles in the chocolate and half in the hazelnuts. Return to the baking tray, cover with non-stick baking paper and chill in the fridge for 1–2 hours, or until firm. Store in an airtight container in the fridge for up to 5 days.

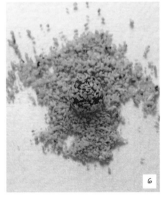

Lemon and white chocolate creams

Makes: 12
Prep: 40 minutes
Cook: 5-10 minutes
Set: 13-18 hours

For an Oriental twist on these decadent truffles, add a large pinch of ground cardamom seeds and star anise to the cream and chocolate mixture.

300 g/10½ oz white chocolate, roughly chopped

2 tbsp double cream

finely grated rind of 1 lemon

2 tbsp limoncello

55 g/2 oz unsalted butter, softened and diced

25 g/1 oz pistachio nuts, finely chopped

1. Put 100 g/3½ oz chocolate and all the cream in a heatproof bowl, set the bowl over a saucepan of gently simmering water and heat until melted.

2. Remove from the heat, add the lemon rind, limoncello and butter and whisk for 3–4 minutes, or until thickened. Transfer to an airtight container and chill in the fridge for 6–8 hours, or until firm.

3. Line a baking tray with non-stick baking paper. Scoop teaspoonfuls of the mixture and, using the palms of your hands, roll them into truffle-sized balls. Place the balls on the prepared tray, cover with cling film and freeze for 6–8 hours.

4. Put the remaining chocolate in a heatproof bowl, set the bowl over a saucepan of gently simmering water and heat until melted. Using 2 forks, dip each truffle into the chocolate to coat evenly. Return them to the prepared baking tray, sprinkle over the pistachios and chill in the fridge for 1–2 hours, or until firm. Store in an airtight container in the fridge for up to 5 days.

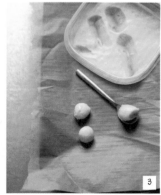

Espresso truffles

Makes: 12
Prep: 40 minutes
Cook: 5–10 minutes
Set: 13–18 hours

For a twist on these coffee truffles, simply replace the coffee with Irish Bailey's Cream liqueur or any orange-flavoured liqueur such as Grand Marnier or Cointreau.

300 g/10½ oz plain chocolate, roughly chopped

2 tbsp double cream

1 tbsp strong espresso coffee, cooled

2 tbsp coffee liqueur

55 g/2 oz unsalted butter, softened and diced

edible gold leaf, to decorate (optional)

1. Put 100 g/3½ oz chocolate and all the cream in a heatproof bowl, set the bowl over a saucepan of gently simmering water and heat until melted.

2. Remove from the heat, add the espresso, coffee liqueur and butter and whisk for 3–4 minutes, or until thickened. Transfer to an airtight container and chill in the fridge for 6–8 hours, or until firm.

3. Line a baking tray with non-stick baking paper. Scoop teaspoonfuls of the mixture and, using the palms of your hands, roll them into truffle-sized balls. Place the balls on the prepared tray, cover with cling film and freeze for 6–8 hours.

4. Put the remaining chocolate in a heatproof bowl, set the bowl over a saucepan of gently simmering water and heat until melted. Using 2 forks, dip each truffle into the chocolate to coat evenly. Return them to the prepared baking tray and chill in the fridge for 1–2 hours, or until firm. Top each truffle with edible gold paper to decorate, if desired. Store in an airtight container in the fridge for up to 5 days.

Chilli and cardamom chocolate thins

Makes: 40
Prep: 30 minutes
Cook: 5-10 minutes
Set: 1-2 hours

These simple treats are perfect for kids to make. They're ideal for putting into a pretty box and giving as a present too.

CHILLI PLAIN CHOCOLATE THINS

200 g/7 oz plain chocolate, roughly chopped

a large pinch of hot chilli powder

edible glitter, to decorate

CARDAMOM WHITE CHOCOLATE THINS

200 g/7 oz white chocolate, roughly chopped

½ tsp cardamom seeds, crushed

25 g/1 oz pistachio nuts, finely chopped, plus extra to decorate

edible glitter, to decorate

1. Line 4 baking trays with non-stick baking paper.

2. For the chilli plain chocolate thins, put the plain chocolate in a heatproof bowl, set the bowl over a saucepan of gently simmering water and heat until melted. Remove from the heat and stir in the chilli powder.

3. Drop teaspoonfuls of the chocolate mixture onto 2 of the prepared baking trays. Scatter over a little edible glitter before the chocolate sets. Leave to set in a cool place, but not in the fridge, for 1-2 hours.

4. For the cardamom white chocolate thins, put the white chocolate in a heatproof bowl, set the bowl over a saucepan of gently simmering water and heat until melted. Remove from the heat and stir in the cardamom and pistachios.

5. Drop teaspoonfuls of the white chocolate mixture onto the remaining 2 prepared baking trays. Scatter over the remaining chopped pistachios and a little edible glitter before the chocolate sets. Leave to set in a cool place, but not in the fridge, for 1-2 hours. Store in an airtight container in a cool, dry place for up to 5 days.

Mini macaroons

Makes: 20
Prep: 1¼ hours
Cook: 30–35 minutes
Set: 1–2 hours

Weigh and measure your ingredients carefully when making these delectable macaroons, as it is crucial to get the proportions right.

125 g/4½ oz icing sugar, sifted

125 g/4½ oz ground almonds

2 large egg whites (weighing 90 g/3¼ oz)

110 g/3¾ oz caster sugar

3 tbsp water

a few drops of pink food colouring

BUTTERCREAM

140 g/5 oz unsalted butter, softened

280 g/10 oz icing sugar, sifted

1–2 tbsp milk

a few drops of vanilla extract

1. Preheat the oven to 150°C/300°F/Gas Mark 2. Line 3 large baking trays with non-stick baking paper.

2. Put the sifted icing sugar, almonds and 40 g/2½ oz egg whites into a large mixing bowl and mix to a paste using a wooden spoon.

3. Put the caster sugar and water into a small heavy-based saucepan. Heat gently for 5 minutes, until the sugar has dissolved, tilting the pan to mix the ingredients together. Increase the heat and boil rapidly for 12–15 minutes, or until the mixture reaches 115°C/240°F on a sugar thermometer, goes syrupy and thickens.

4. Whisk the remaining egg white in a large, clean mixing bowl until you have stiff, moist-looking peaks, then gradually whisk in the hot syrup until the mixure is shiny. Spoon this into the almond paste and stir together gently until the mixture becomes stiff and shiny again. Add the pink food colouring, then mix well.

5. Spoon the mixture into a piping bag fitted with a 1-cm/½-inch nozzle and pipe 40 x 2-cm/¾-inch circles onto the prepared baking trays, about 2 cm/¾ inches apart. Leave to stand for 30 minutes, or until a skin forms. Bake in the preheated oven for 12–15 minutes, with the door slightly ajar, until firm.

6. For the buttercream, put the butter in a large mixing bowl and beat until soft. Add half the sifted icing sugar and beat until smooth. Add the remaining icing sugar, 1 tablespoon of the milk and all the vanilla extract and beat until creamy. Add a little extra icing sugar to thicken or milk to make it runnier, if needed. Spoon the mixture into a piping bag fitted with a large star nozzle.

7. Transfer the macaroons, still on their paper, to a wire rack. Leave to cool for 1–2 hours, then peel off the paper. Pipe a swirl of buttercream on each of half the macaroons and top each with another macaroon.

8. These can be stored without the buttercream in an airtight container in a cool, dry place for up to 5 days.

Mini ginger caramel cookies

Makes: 20
Prep: 1¼ hours
Cook: 30–35 minutes
Set: 1–2 hours

Dulce de leche, or thick caramel paste, is widely available in jars from most good supermarkets and delicatessens. You can use a chocolate and hazelnut spread instead, if you prefer.

1 tsp ground ginger

125 g/4½ oz icing sugar, sifted

125 g/4½ oz ground almonds

2 large egg whites (weighing 90 g/3¾ oz)

110 g/3¾ oz caster sugar

3 tbsp water

10 tbsp caramel (dulce de leche)

1. Preheat the oven to 150°C/300°F/Gas Mark 2. Line 3 large baking trays with non-stick baking paper.

2. Put the ginger, sifted icing sugar, almonds and 40 g/2½ oz egg whites into a large mixing bowl and mix to a paste using a wooden spoon.

3. Put the caster sugar and water into a small heavy-based saucepan. Heat gently for 5 minutes, until the sugar has dissolved, tilting the pan to mix the ingredients together. Increase the heat and boil rapidly for 12–15 minutes, or until the mixture reaches 115°C/240°F on a sugar thermometer, goes syrupy and thickens.

4. Whisk the remaining egg white in a large, clean mixing bowl until you have stiff, moist-looking peaks, then gradually whisk in the hot syrup until the mixture is shiny. Spoon this into the almond paste and stir together gently until the mixture becomes stiff and shiny again.

5. Spoon the mixture into a piping bag fitted with a 1-cm/½-inch nozzle and pipe 40 x 2-cm/¾-inch strips onto the prepared baking trays, about 2 cm/¾ inches apart. Leave to stand for 30 minutes, or until a skin forms. Bake in the preheated oven for 12–15 minutes, with the door slightly ajar, until firm.

6. Transfer the cookies, still on their paper, to a wire rack. Leave to cool for 1–2 hours, then peel off the paper. Drop a teaspoonful of caramel on each of half the cookies and top each with another cookie.

7. These can be stored without the caramel in an airtight container in a cool, dry place for up to 5 days.

Iced citrus marzipan thins

Makes: 30
Prep: 25 minutes
Set: overnight

Originally from Aix-en-Provence in France, these easy-to-make after dinner treats are full of citrus and almond goodness.

200 g/7 oz ground almonds

200 g/7 oz caster sugar

1 large egg

a few drops of citrus extract

finely grated rind of ½ orange

FOR THE ICING

200 g/7 oz fondant icing sugar, sifted, plus extra for dusting

juice of 1 lemon

1. Line a 20-cm/8-inch square baking tin with non-stick baking paper, snipping diagonally into the corners, then pressing the paper into the tin so that the base and sides are lined. Lightly dust a work surface with icing sugar.

2. Put the almonds and caster sugar into a mixing bowl and stir. Add the egg, citrus extract and orange rind and mix, using your hands, to form a stiff paste.

3. Knead the marzipan briefly on the prepared work surface, then press it into the base of the prepared tin using the back of a spoon, until even and smooth. Leave to set for 1 hour.

4. For the icing, put the sifted fondant icing sugar and lemon juice into a mixing bowl and stir until smooth, then spread evenly over the marzipan. Cover and leave in a cool place, but not the fridge, to dry overnight.

5. Cut the iced marzipan into bite-sized shapes of your choice using a fondant or cookie cutter. Store in an airtight container in the fridge for up to 2 days.

Index